The 7 Figure Realtor™

Become a Mega Marketer, Sustain Mega Income & Experience Mega Success

Joey Fenwick

ISBN-13:978-1530665488
ISBN-10:1530665485

PUBLISHED BY:
10-10-10 PUBLISHING
MARKHAM, ON
CANADA

Contents

Acknowledgements

I would like to say Thank You to a number of people who helped me put this concept forward and, more importantly, helped provide the motivation and vehicle to get it done.

Jeff Vacek and his team, who planted the seed in my head and started this idea back in 2009.

Brendon Burchard, speaking and writing mentor, and Miriam Cohen, who did such a great job at pulling data from my brain and helping me put it together in a simple way.

Action Coach for all the training and confidence to push me to challenge myself and grow in new ways that I never thought possible.

My friends, Sean Conway, Eric Wolfe, Darrell Ellis and my family, Jeanne Wall, Janie Berry, Teri Ross and Hunter Fenwick who gave me support, a lot of patience and help in order to get this project off the ground and come together for others to share.

Lastly, to my kids, RJ, Alexis and Tristan who sacrificed "mommy time" that was wanted and needed so that I could follow my dreams and continue moving forward in life and business. I love you all!

Foreword

As a Real Estate Agent, you know that the business has its ups and downs. It can be subject to changes in the economy and experience slow periods based on the time of year. You may even find yourself wondering if there is any hope of building a truly viable business long-term or rediscovering the passion you once had for being a Real Estate Agent. If so, *The 7 Figure Realtor© Marketing System* will quickly become your go-to guide for creating and maintaining a robust Real Estate business that thrives under any economic circumstances.

In this book, Mega Real Estate Agent and Coach Joey Fenwick has laid out the steps to take and the tools to use to make your own business a consistent and significant money maker. After reading this book, and integrating her words of wisdom into your daily business, you will soon see your income double, triple or more.

As you'll see, some of the old tried and true ways of marketing your business are no longer sufficient in this digital age. Fenwick knows which ones to keep, which to update and which ones to let fall by the wayside. She answers all your questions and many you likely haven't known to ask. And, Fenwick explains all the new digital tools and shows you how easy they are to use and how they will help you develop and implement a mega-marketing plan that will make you a Real Estate superstar.

Whether you are a new Agent or have been in Real Estate for decades, the author's mega-marketing program will open your eyes to a new level of success. You will learn how to generate a consistent income stream, with fresh, motivated prospects — both sellers and buyers.

Get ready to fall in love with your Real Estate business all over again.

Raymond Aaron
New York Times Best Selling Author

Introduction

Despite your best efforts, does it ever feel like you're wondering where your next client is coming from, just waiting for potential homebuyers to call? Are your tried and true methods for generating leads not producing anymore? What works today is already obsolete for tomorrow. Or, does your business fluctuate from nicely busy to painfully slow? If so, do you ever have moments when you are afraid that you really don't know how to get more business and market yourself?

Don't be discouraged. You are definitely not alone. Many Real Estate Agents find themselves in the same position. Like most of them, you are probably tired of the effect the economy always seems to have on your business, as well as the fact that your business keeps changing even faster than technology. And, that's not to mention the normal stresses and inconsistencies of just being in Real Estate.

First, you need to stop being a Lone Ranger. If you doubt it, look at some scary facts about today's Real Estate market:

- Approximately 7,000 Real Estate agents' businesses were expected to fail in 2013.

- Agents in the first two years of business average only $9,700 a year and many of them don't survive.

- The average Agent has been in business for 15 years and earns an average of $43,000 a year. They often need a second job to make ends meet.

- Even Agents who have been in the business for 16 years and up average only $57,500 a year in income.

At the same time, despite the financial and market fluctuations, there is always a select group of Real Estate agents who are constantly busy, generating sales for clients and income for themselves. And, they are doing so on all kinds of deals, not just high-end luxury homes or below market investor flips that are supposed to be economy-proof. How do they do it? How do they have an up market all the time?

They're Real Estate Mega-Marketers, that's how. And you can be one too.

It's time to stop worrying and start marketing your business for mega results. If you're ready to build a successful Real Estate business that continues to expand and become more profitable, but don't know where to start, this book is for you.

Developing systems that continuously generate warm leads and convert them into qualified, ready to go sellers and buyers is the key to your success. I know. I've been doing just that for more than 21 years. As an award-winning mortgage lender and Real

Estate Agent, I have honed my sales and marketing abilities to build a team of Mega-Marketing Real Estate Agents who help their clients make money by selling or finding homes of their dreams.

What my Mega-Marketing Agents understand is that the Real Estate market has changed in the last ten to fifteen years, and it keeps changing at record speeds. Agents have more tools in their toolboxes than ever before, and it is critical to understand what those tools do, which of them is most effective and how to use them together to build a successful business.

For example, prospective buyers shop differently today. The Internet has become an integral part of marketing and has empowered buyers to find properties on their own, without even calling or walking into a Real Estate Agent's office. It has, therefore, become critical to create an online presence that has you seen in the right places by the right people. And, that doesn't mean just putting up a branding website. Your website and social media have to be alive and breathing daily.

Also, there is more competition than ever before. People are more entrepreneurial than ever before, especially women, and they are entering Real Estate because it affords them the perfect opportunity to control their careers and create a manageable work/life balance. You need to be sharp and creative. You need to be generating leads consistently and cultivating them before another agent can pull them away. I will show you how to crush your competition and how to determine which marketing systems to kill and which ones to put more money into.

Having been the owner or manager of multiple successful businesses, including Real Estate and Mortgage companies, I understand the challenges, pressures and pleasures associated with being an executive and an owner. As a Real Estate agent with a team, I have identified the marketing and management tools that create constant growth. And, as a coach, I've been teaching Real Estate Agents and other self-employed businesspeople how to build their businesses through target marketing both online and off, lead generation, the use of automated systems and winning sales techniques.

When I looked around and saw how many quality Real Estate agents were missing out on the business they deserved, I saw a need to share what I have learned over the years with a wider audience. That's why I decided to write this book. It's a guide to making your business more successful by adopting new tools to meet today's marketing needs. It's also about managing your leads and your business more efficiently and effectively for continuous growth (without it consuming you and your time).

In this book, you'll also learn about crystallizing your vision, setting objectives for your business, identifying the right target audience and employing streetwise marketing. With respect to the Internet, there are simple how-to's for search engine optimization, successfully using Facebook and Linked In and leveraging videos. (You will learn how to get each of your listings on the front page of Google in no time!) You will also find easy-to-use strategies and systems for managing the other online components of your marketing, improving referral marketing and follow-up, and streamlining the backend of your business.

In sum, you are about to see why marketing the right way, networking with other professionals and knowing your numbers are a must. You will also come to understand why having integrity and caring about others ties it all together into a profitable business. Most importantly, you will start to think like a marketer – a Mega-Marketer.

Imagine getting in front of three to five new qualified buyers and sellers each and every month. You will see an immediate impact on your business, as well as a steadier stream of potential buyers and sellers. Your conversion and closing rates will increase, and your confidence will rise. Now, you will never again have to worry about finding business.

Are you ready to take your Real Estate business to another level?If so, be certain you are ready to do this with me. Write down your answers to some critical questions:

- ***What is driving you to create a more consistent income with less time spent working?*** In other words, what do you want **TO HAVE?** What will you do with the extra money and time? Is it that you want to be a more involved parent, have a hobby you haven't had enough time to pursue fully or is it as simple as wanting to commit to going to the gym on a regular basis?

- ***Who do you need TO BE in order to achieve your goals and a balanced life?*** Do you know what you need to have, talk like, or look like to be the person you need to be to have a mega-successful Real Estate business?

- ***What do you need TO DO to make this happen?*** You will learn a lot of laser-like strategies in this book, but you might not have to do everything to be successful. Understanding the Return on Investment of every activity is critical. So is determining what needs to get done and who has to do it. Often, you will find delegation is one of the most useful and profitable tools in your toolbox.

Now put all of these answers together and you will get one of the key formulas to setting your goals and crafting the ideal business and marketing plan for your life. This simple formula for ultimate success is:

Be x Do = Have

Notice that you start by determining what you want to have, and then work backward to get there. Makes sense, doesn't it? After all, if you are not shooting for a meaningful goal, why do anything at all?

Chapter One
Being Visible & Loving It

In today's rapidly changing Real Estate market, being visible has taken on a whole new meaning. There was a time, not too far in the past, when getting seen was a relatively easy thing to accomplish. It literally meant immersing yourself in community organizations, knowing your neighbors and their children by name, running small ads in the local newspapers and posting personalized for-sale signs on the properties you were representing. Those old rules just aren't enough anymore, not in this Internet driven, buyer-empowered environment.

Getting Seen

Being seen by the right people is still the ultimate goal for a Real Estate Agent, but belonging to key Real Estate business organizations, attending alumni groups or participating in the local Chamber of Commerce will no longer suffice. Today your neighbors and Real Estate industry colleagues are on their smart phones and computers more than they are at business lunches or monthly get-togethers. Potential clients once looked exclusively for personal referrals; now 90% of them turn to the Internet for everything, including where to find their dream home or next investment.

What does that mean for you? First, don't cancel those group or community memberships. They are still valuable, just not valuable enough on their own. Next, rethink the definition of "location, location, location." Today's Real Estate Agents must have an Internet presence that is equal to their in-person, face-to-face one. Start making your face and your business visible on the web, especially where your best prospects are searching for their new homes. Location does still matter as people copy and follow others, so finding the popular 'hot spots' locally will also help. Later in this book, you'll learn where on the Internet you should be, and how to maximize your exposure by using marketing techniques that place you at the top of your prospects' Google ranking. Remember, if you are not on the first few pages, you aren't there at all. People search globally yet still buy locally.

The 'Right People' for You

To build your Brand and your business (I'll get to the differences between the two in another chapter), you'll need to determine where your greatest marketing and business-building opportunities lie. Defining your 'target audience' is the first step in making your business more efficient and effective because knowing who represents the greatest potential for your business will significantly impact where you want to be seen and by whom. The three questions to ask yourself are:

- "Who is my best business prospect?"

- "Who else represents a significant business opportunity for me?"

- "Who do I want to work with?"

Think of it this way. There are a set number of hot qualified leads out there at one time. Why work harder and market more to capture them from the general population when you can do less and achieve the same or better results by targeting certain groups and places? That's what happens when you focus your efforts on the right people for you.

Of course, there is always some possibility that you may need to have the broadest offerings in your area in order to differentiate yourself from your competition, but it is much more likely that narrowing your target audience by concentrating on a particular niche will be significantly better for your business. And, zeroing in on your target audience first is critical because it affects everything about how you develop your business and your marketing plan.

Consider all the alternatives based on the types of Real Estate and the demographics of the area in which you do business. (In a later chapter, you will see how MLS can help you do this quickly and efficiently.) In addition to economic considerations, like household income, learn all you can about the lifestyle characteristics of recent buyers and sellers.

In addition, it is important to identify what is distinctive about the area in which you want to concentrate: school rankings, home sizes, the amount of new construction taking place, entertainment and cultural resources, hospitals and other medical services, etc. Knowing all this will help narrow your target audience by family size, number of children, age and leisure activities.

For example, your area might be attracting young families with children because of the great schools and availability of larger-sized homes. Then again, the best target for your business might be retirees who have a passion for golf. Consider what makes one neighborhood better than another for these buyers. In the case of those older empty nesters, the perfect easier maintenance house won't just need to be near the golf course; they will be looking for first-class hospitals or 50+ communities as well.

Also, know your strengths and consider them when refining your target audience. Ask your current and past clients what they think is your special expertise, the thing that makes you unique or, at the very least, superior to your competition. Is it the listings you have or the way you walk people through the buying and selling process? Perhaps you have a specific interest in helping first-time buyers and current clients love the way you 'hold their hand' during each part of the process. If the thing that makes you special dovetails with who is currently buying within your community, then that's the bulls-eye for your business. It's the niche where business opportunity and your Unique Selling Proposition (USP) can come together.

Remember, it is only when you truly love what you do that you can really soar!

On the other hand, perhaps your best prospects are buyers looking to trade up to the coveted luxury market as they achieve a new level of economic success, or parents who need more room for a growing family. Again, it's critical to ask yourself these questions and decide where your talents and interests lie. Know which target can help you generate the most fun as well as business success.

The principles, strategies and tactics in later chapters will teach you how to stake out your own viable niche within the Real Estate market.

Branding Your Business

Your Brand is your reputation. It's how people see your business. You've just read why it is critical to know how you are perceived by past and current clients. It's also vitally important to know how prospective clients see you and your business. What they think of you, how they view your services and expertise defines your Brand too. You want prospective clients to think of you the way your satisfied clients do.

Image, on the other hand, is what you say about your business. It's what you promise potential clients and how you deliver on that promise. Your image is the face you put on your business, and it must be part of all your marketing efforts.

Mega-successful Real Estate businesses control their branding by performing in line with the image they create and promote. Trouble arises when your image and your Brand are not the same. No matter what marketing position you take, no matter what image you try to convey, if others don't see your business the way you want them to, you have a branding problem. But, that problem has a solution. You have a chance to change people's opinions.

As a Mega-Marketer you can determine how you want to be seen, especially when you know exactly to whom you are talking, and what information is most motivating for them. By creating and marketing your image, you will be able to build a mega-brand that will bring your business significant and long-term growth. In other words, you'll learn how to go beyond just being seen, to being well-branded , extraordinarily well-branded. You'll get there through marketing a meaningful image that makes you unique in the Real Estate industry in your area.

Creating Your Image

Your image will position you as the best Real Estate Agent for your target audience. Do your research, know what prospective clients want most from an Agent, and identify those business strengths that give those buyers (or sellers) what they are looking for: are you a great negotiator, do you only show clients exactly what they're looking for or are you known for handling out-of-the-ordinary properties, and so on. The more you can establish yourself as the perfect match for a key segment of the market, the more you will stand out versus your competition, and the more you will be able to establish yourself as 'the expert', 'the best' or 'the authority' in your area.

Not Online? You're Nowhere

In my 21-plus-year career, I've achieved a tremendous amount of success based on my ability to adapt constantly to the pace of technology. Its far-reaching effect on our industry is undeniable. To duplicate my success you too must embrace the Internet with open arms. Don't be afraid. The Internet can seem intimidating, but you'll learn how to tame it, build engaging websites and use social media like a pro.

Having a superior online presence doesn't have to be complicated. This book will teach you how to use technology to grow your business with the utmost simplicity. But, you must be open and willing to change. You won't get anything from my proven roadmap if you don't want to grow, or refuse to learn and implement new ideas like online marketing. Make the jump and become a Mega-Real Estate Marketer. You could double or triple your business ... or more.

Recap

- The Real Estate market has evolved along with technological advancements. You must keep pace.

- Prospective buyers rely on the Internet 92% of the time in their initial searches for their next area and home.

- If you're not where they are looking, you can't be found.

- Mega-Marketers narrow in on a Real Estate target buyer for greater success.

- Branding is what people say about your business. If you are Coca-Cola and have millions of dollars to tell the world to follow you, great. But, if you are a small business owner like a Realtor, then you don't have that kind of budget and therefore need to take the educational marketing approach. What this means is you must target your market, give them free education about what they want to learn about, and give it to them in a unique fashion with ongoing follow-up so that when they want to buy you are the professional, the knowledgeable one and also the one who shows the ultimate value.
- Your image is what you say about your business. When it doesn't match your Brand, you need to take control of your Brand and fix it.

Chapter Two
Mega-Marketing for Real Estate

If you are ready to launch your Real Estate business to the next level, one of the first things you need to do is stop putting "all your eggs in one basket." Most Agents and brokers heavily rely on referrals. That means months of feast and months of famine. Plus, the Real Estate market doesn't work that way anymore.

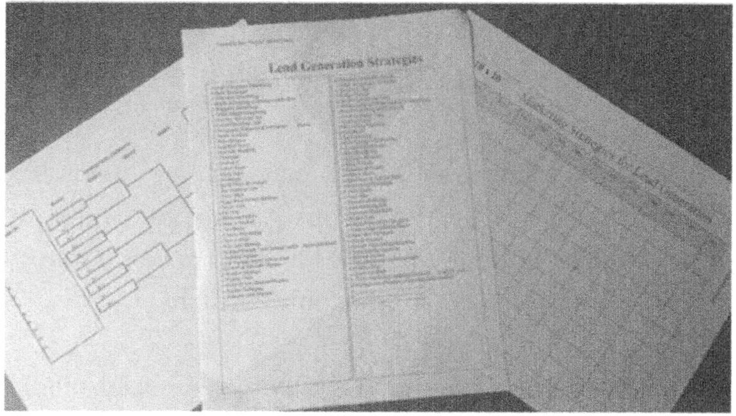

Mega-Marketers develop multiple streams of lead generation. Don't rely on one marketing technique or venue to generate all of your sales. Diversify your marketing efforts so that you get seen in all the right places by your target. You must be found everywhere and create ten funnels of leads coming from ten different sources.

Mega-Marketing by the Numbers

The secret to success is, in large part, simple math. By focusing your efforts and time for maximum return, you can catapult your Real Estate business into a steady revenue-producing machine. It's about managing your efforts for maximum productivity and building a steady stream of potential clients (buyers and sellers). To some extent, sellers are the most valuable leads because you need to have many options for buyers.

These are the key proven techniques for generating steady mega results:

10 x 10

Cultivate ten marketing sources so that each represents 10% of your business. That way, if one source is not performing well, the others will still be bringing in leads and business on a regular basis. That's how to keep your income constant.

Think about dividing your efforts between social media – primarily Facebook and Linked In— client referrals, community groups, your eProperty sites, your own website, You Tube, print or on-air advertising, mailers, community newsletters, etc. Find your avenues of greatest potential, i.e. where your target prospects are, and focus on those sources. Build or expand your Internet options first as they are likely your least developed resources to date. As you implement your Mega-Marketing plan, you will be able to track the results of each resource and refine your marketing efforts for greater Return on Investment (ROI).

Your 90 Day Plan

Three months – that's all it takes once you start using my proven systems for eliminating obstacles and time wasters. In 90 days, you'll implement strategies that will green-light your day and get you in the groove. Just focus progressively on each aspect of the plan that follows, starting with "completing a skill/fun chart," then getting organized in all aspects of your business, from accounting to recruiting a new team.

The 50/50 Split

It's easy to get caught up in today's sales, but what about tomorrow's revenue? The bottom line is that steady lead generation is key to growing your Real Estate business. To make that happen, you must allocate your resources 50/50, prospecting to sales. In other words, half of your activities and/or time should focus on prospecting while the other half is used for the remainder of your business functions.

A creative mix of daily and weekly activities equals results, so remember that you should always be generating leads. Don't get too busy focusing on the details of current sales or daily operations. You will soon have automated systems that streamline your office backend, and will be making more money so you can hire others to do paperwork. Your primary purpose is to be marketing your business – only you can do that. Marketing, in the end, must be your primary focus if you want to soar like an eagle.

Online and Local

You also need to recognize that there is such a thing as online local efforts. Most people think the Internet is only national in its reach, which would mean a lot of wasted resources spent outside your target audience. But, that's just not true! A lot of online sites are extremely neighborhood-focused, centered on local activities, school rankings and distributing local newspaper content electronically. Even in a huge city like New York, there are a lot of localized websites.

For example, Ditmasparkcorner.com is a private blog/newsletter focusing on features and advertising for a group of neighborhoods on the south side of Prospect Park in the borough of Brooklyn, New York. In your area that probably translates into a website that focuses on a sub-segment or two of one housing development. And, there are individual websites like this for almost every community in the country.

There are also networks of localized listings and websites like Birminghampatch.com, which services an upscale community in Oakland County, Michigan. It is part of "a community-specific news, information and engagement platform" owned by AOL. Like many localized social sites, these blogs include a guide to neighborhood businesses, including Real Estate and Financial Services. A simple Google search for activities within your area will help you find the right localized online resources for your Real Estate business.

Local websites love to support business owners in their area as those businesses provide the sites' primary sources of income. Promotion goes both ways so, in addition to getting listed (make sure that both your hottest properties and your agency are included), help generate news for these sites. Enhance your reputation as the Real Estate expert in your area by making friends with the editors and bloggers, submitting helpful hints on buying or selling your home and, in general, by becoming their go-to person for everything Real Estate.

The Top Five Online Marketing Strategies

1. ***Create your own identity online with a business website.***

   Make it easy for potential clients to learn about you and your business (Branding), as well as to get in touch with you via their medium of choice. Include free offers on your site that educate the public, advance the deal and pre-sell your Real Estate agency without having to get a Real Estate Agent involved. Save face-to-face and phone contact for your hottest, ready-to-buy prospects.

2. ***Develop a steady presence on social media.***

   Create a Facebook business page and leverage Linked In to develop a following and generate leads. (Interesting, Twitter's okay, but it doesn't get the same type of results that Facebook does.) This is today's no-brainer for success in Real Estate. All it takes is a little online socializing and a lot of educating. Offering free information in return for an email address is one of the best lead generation tactics out there.

   These are also great vehicles for announcing new listings or completed sales. It is important to project your Brand in your posts and include non-self promotional information. The key to social media is to connect on a personal level. If you are not sure what to post about, remember the acronym FORM. You may have heard the term before, especially if you have taken courses on how to network successfully. It stands for the subjects that everyone can relate to and talk about: Family, Occupation, Recreation, and Money. You can link to your business blog, support local charity events and otherwise cement your relationship with the community.

3. ***Use the right keywords and organic Search Engine Optimization (SEO) techniques to make Google's first page.***

   These are essential online marketing strategies for being seen. While you can pay for advertising, what you really want in today's online world is to be found for free before your competitors are found. This is accomplished through organic SEO. The term organic applies to non-advertising mentions like on your website, in blogs, listings and social media posts. Searchers often give these organic search results greater credence than paid promotional space (as they do a mention in newspaper or magazine content versus self-promotions like a print ad).

It's a much simpler concept than it might seem at first glance. Learn what terms your prospects use when searching for information by reading the Google analysis. You can also ask new prospects for anecdotal information. The more you know about the search terms prospects use, the easier it will be build content using the right words and phrases in your online content.

These search terms are called keywords or keyword phrases. You may also hear or see the term long-tailed keyword, which simply means that it is a phrase rather than an individual word. Long-tailed keywords are especially useful in targeting within your niche of the Real Estate business.

Google and other search engines, like Bing and Yahoo, scan websites for these words and then use a mathematical formula to determine what's displayed first, second, third, etc. in the results. The more places your Real Estate business is associated with those words or phrases, the more times Google will pick you up when it scans. (There's a bit more to it, but you get the picture.) The individual pages of your website are counted separately; so are your property listings.

Do you know the five key Real Estate search terms you need to get your Real Estate listing on the first page of Google? The top ones are usually related to Subdivision, City, Zip Code, High School and Elementary School. Other subjects people search for are entertainment and lifestyle activities. Keywords work, and it only takes 20 minutes or so to post!

Later in this book, you'll also learn more about the power of Facebook – it gets billions of hits! Yes, billions!! So does You Tube and, for higher income clients, Linked In. On average, Linked In members make $112,000 a year and Facebook participants only $61,000. That can make a real difference to your business, especially when your listings are in the luxury market.

When you are talking about keywords for your industry, keep in mind that the more specific you are, the better. "Real Estate" may get the biggest monthly volume of hits, but that just makes it harder to get to page one of an Internet search. It's by narrowing your search terms to find your hottest prospects that you will get a high Google ranking. Plus, it makes for the generation of more qualified leads. Keep getting more specific and watch your rankings soar.

4. ***Advertising works.***

There was a time before the Internet and social media when paid advertising was everything, but those paid announcements appeared on TV and radio, in print and on billboards. Ads are still important, and many are still in the same types of media. But, in today's Internet-based market, the most important thing an advertiser needs to know is "where did they find you?"

There are four things every ad needs:

1. A targeted audience

2. 'What's In It For Me' (WIIFM) content that is relative to your target prospect

3. A unique WIIFM promise or claim

4. An offer with a call to action (CTA)

In terms of targeting your ad, you need to place it around the right keywords wherever your target audience searches for related subjects. For instance, placement may be within school rankings or announcements of cultural and community activities.

Be sure to send ad responders to the right place, whether it is to your business website or ActiveRain blog (to collect your informational offer) or to a specific listing for an update on its availability. Or, you may direct people to a page of your website that sorts listings by school district. On the other hand, if you are targeting seniors or DINKS (dual income, no kids), you might provide a list of cultural events, shopping by area, etc.

5. ***Become a regular blogger.***

In Real Estate blogging, all you really need to know is this: use the blogging platform called ActiveRain. It's an online platform for anything and everything relating to Real Estate. By using their simple blogging platform, you can ensure your listings will end up on the first page of Google. Why? Because Google likes ActiveRain Rain Makers!

The site brings a constant flow of education to users from industry leaders who share their secrets and marketing ideas. ActiveRain was built specifically for the Real Estate industry, so all two million+ members are Real Estate Agents or in related fields. ActiveRain has over four and one-half million web pages to date and adds about 2,000 per day, and almost every blog post is, in some way, related to Real Estate. Since every blog (webpage) on ActiveRain stays under the ActiveRain.com umbrella, they all add up to one tremendous Google set of Google rankings. You need to be part of this family!

What Should You Blog About?

Remember FORM and your keywords. Do your research and see what other topics ActiveRain bloggers are writing about. Check your Google results to see which links are directing the most prospects to your business site. Hang in, and you'll soon find out the top five things to blog about to get you on the first page of a Google search. How cool is that?

Recap

- FEAR (False Expectations Appearing Real) often keeps realtors where they are.

- Once you get the elements of your 90-day plan underway, prepare to watch your business soar. You'll wonder why you were ever stuck in what we call the fear or victim mode — blaming others (the economy, the marketplace or unrealistic clients), using excuses and, in general, being in denial about why your strategies aren't working.

- Know the new Real Estate marketing math — 10 x 10 for multiple sources of leads and revenue and 50/50 focus between marketing and sales.

- Local online websites rock. They're everywhere, and your target uses them. You must be there too.

- Build a website for your business, but don't stop there. Your Google ranking depends, in part, on how many mentions come up in a search. For discounts and VIP treatment, learn more at www.ifoundagent.com/action-coach. It's a top website for Real Estate Agents.

- Take advantage of websites with clout, like ActiveRain and eProperty websites.

- Know the right keywords and phrases. Use them in website content, advertisements and blog posts. Analyze what works work best.

- Don't forget about paid advertising, both online and off. Always include a CTA and uniquely said WIIFM claims.

Congratulations on choosing the victor mode, with the qualities of ownership, accountability and responsibility. Get ready to win!

Chapter Three

Building Your Mega-Marketing Plan

It's wonderful that you've made the decision to hitch your future to the star of Mega-Marketing. You've already seen why it's a smart decision. And you know I'll be with you all the way, walking you through the process in the pages of this book.

So, now it's time to put it all together and start getting mega results.

Getting Started

You need to kick off your plan by choosing your 10 x 10 – the ten different sources that will generate your leads going forward. We've talked about some of the possible ways you can go, from social media to your own website, community groups, You Tube and Craig's List.

You need a mix of online and offline, local and national sources and at least one social media site – I recommend Facebook for its billions of hits. An active business website that gets updated with new content frequently is a must (you'll learn how to create a rocking one in Chapter Four). In the next chapter, you will also learn how to use ePropertySites.com to maximize your presence on the web. Other sure-fire hits to consider are Angie's List, hot videos online and, again, blogging on ActiveRain.

What should you say?

Next, you need to create a USP and guarantees that offer prospects a no-risk proposition. Simply put, your USP is a statement about what makes you better than your competition. What is it that you offer that others can't match?

To create your USP don't try to cover all the bases. It is exhausting and, instead of making you a Superman or Superwoman, it makes you weak in all areas. So, figure out where you have the best reputation and what that means for your clients. Then, focus on it in your content and marketing materials. You will find that zeroing in on your strengths pumps up your energy as well as your visibility.

If you have trouble identifying a USP for your business, keep in mind that, in addition to representing the word "selling," the S in USP can also stand for Service and Statistics. So, your marketing can refer to how you sell, the way you service clients, and business results statistics that wow the public. Start making a list of the things that make you stand out in all three of these areas.

To pinpoint further the strengths you want to use in your marketing, utilize MLS, the multiple listing service for Real Estate brokers in your area. You've likely worked with MLS already with regard to appraisals and listing information, but the data it collects can also help you gauge your standing versus competitors; pull out statistics that will impress your clients.

Also, take a serious look at trends for a particular neighborhood or target audience. There is a wonderful example of how to use MLS data later on in this chapter, and all sample forms can be found in the Appendix, MLS search forms 1-5.

What type of guarantee should you offer?

Once you get a statistical handle on an area with high potential, it's time to choose your guarantees. Don't be afraid to make promises to both buyers and sellers. Need an example? Try using statistics to find the average timeframe for making a sale in your area, add a safety net of another week or month and offer an "I will find your dream home for you in five weeks or less."

For sellers, the line changes a bit, and you'll want to add an "or" – as in "Or I'll buy it." (That may sound a bit outrageous, but boy would it set you apart from your competition). If that's too scary an offer for you, try letting the client cancel their listing at any time if they're unsatisfied. Create a guarantee that works for you and promises something you know you have the expertise to deliver! Don't forget to set restrictions and make it clear exactly what has to happen for you to keep the guarantee (readiness to show, ability to have open houses, etc.).

How local should you go?

Depending where you live and work, you may be able to narrow your geographical focus down to a subdivision or two. Use MLS information on Actives and Under Contract within the last 90-days to analyze which part of your area has the highest potential for your Real Estate business. Start with the largest denominator you have, probably zip codes, and work your way in, looking at housing developments, subdivisions, etc.

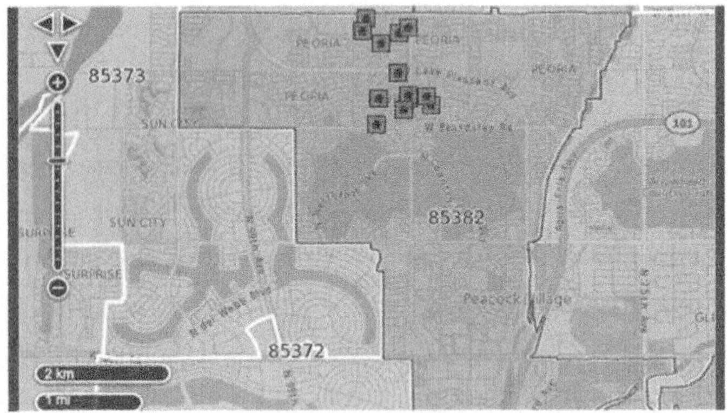

Next check the four to six-month trends to see if the area is getting hotter or cooling off. (See MLS forms 2 and 3 in the Appendix for examples.)

Determine the 'hot pockets' of activity and compare their potential based on the number of houses in the location, average selling price, remaining potential inventory, etc. Remember that you have a close goal of at least three properties per month, and factor that objective into the data.

Marketing Campaign Step # 1 –
Choose Your Target Effectively With Up-to-Date Research
Use ARMLS – Quick Search for data – Compare 2-3 Zip Codes –
Rounding Down to 3-5 Subdivisions to Find Best Most Active Subdivisions

Target Market Data for ______________________
(Timeframe and Marketing)

Active & UCB / Pending & Closed from __________ **to** ___________
(Dates no more than 1 to 3 months old)

Price Range Zipcode / Subdivision	150K-300K	300K-450K	450K-600K	600K-750k	>750k
85382 * This zip better	99 266		1) Analyze data – 1% listed – 1.7% sold – Camino	Good sub has turnover of 9-10% regularly, check history	
85381	46 116		0.9% listed to 2.6% sold in Dove Valley	** This one needs listings more demand.	
Camino A Lago	5 8		2) * Now map search & mail to area where other homes listed in sub	3) Check #'s 4-6 mos, is it going up or down in #'s	
Dove Valley Ranch	13 35		4) Look for pricing jump for headline	5) Decide how to market – DM, postcard, fliers, D2D	
# of homes in each sub	Camino 515 Dove 1341		6) Write effective marketing WIIFM?		
Ask list of ???'s to Rt					

- Choose 2-3 zip codes in areas & determine price range to target
- Choose top squares, click subdivision (ascending) & choose top 3-5
- Get # of homes in sub in tax record/ To determine which #'s are best
- Value change 1-3 mos vs 3-6 mos for headlines or direction of homes

For example, assume that there are two hot subdivisions, one with three listings and six closed, the other with four listings and seven closed. Since both subdivisions look good, you may not easily realize which is best. But, if you check the tax records you'll see how many homes are in each subdivision. That will allow you to determine the true ratios for open and sold so you can see how hot each of the subdivisions actually is.

Once you have analyzed all the data, your greatest geographical opportunity will become obvious. Just be sure to review all the statistics, check the trends and take a preliminary look at breakeven/ROI on the cost of marketing materials.

Then, be certain that this geographical area is one you can dominate. Double check that the demographics and lifestyle characteristics match your skills and the things you most like to do, the ones that make your business fun. Focus on both buyers and sellers. Is the population aging? Might that make for a preponderance of potential sellers? And, are current buyers young couples looking for their first home or couples with children looking for more space? If so, that's definitely a neighborhood with great potential for your business.

Another strategy to keep in mind is focusing on price point and analyzing to find the lowest hanging fruit. In this case, you're targeting properties that are great bargains for your clients.

How can you be prepared when a hot spot cools down?

You will also want to identify nearby areas as they are likely to be the next to get active, especially if demographic and lifestyle considerations are the same as they are in the currently most active 'hot spot' (schools in the same zone, for example, still near a golf course; you get the idea). You will want to begin generating buyer leads in those areas while actively selling in the original 'hot' area.

Know Your Target Audience Inside Out

As you are building your Mega-Marketing plan, it is important to think like your target so you can market where they are most likely to be. Know what they like to do, what they read (online and off), where they shop, what restaurants they go to; in other words, what are the details of their daily lives. These profiles will help you figure out how to reach your audience, both in terms of where to have a presence and what to talk about.

Create Offers That Encourage Face-to-Face Time

In terms of content, review books and movies you know they would love and restaurants they'll thank you for spotlighting. Keep abreast of what's new and point out those things that might particularly be of interest to your target: new tennis courts, upgrades at the public golf course or pool, changes in parking regulations, store openings, etc.

What are the most compelling offers you can make to target clients? You need to ask why someone would work with you. What is in it for them? What are their benefits? Then give it to them. Be unique. The possibilities might include letting young couples with children know about the best schools in the city and targeting great properties nearby that they should be looking at.

Finally, always have a CTA on every platform you use, whether it is Facebook, Craig's List, your website or advertising. The CTA is your final instruction to your reader, so it is clear how they can act immediately. In digital marketing, you can ask for a click. Use a link on your Facebook page, your website or anything online. In fact, you might want to use social media to link people to offers on your website. Use action wordage like "click here and learn how I can help you find your dream home today." Zero in on the right calls to action, and you will set up a steady stream of new clients!

Recap

- Don't rely on one source for all your business (like referrals). It is optimum to have business coming in about equally from ten different sources.

- You need to create a compelling USP (what you want people to think about you). Ask yourself these questions: What are you most knowledgeable about? What do you do better than anyone else? What business activities are the most fun?

- Identify three to five target markets, focusing on geography, demographics, the type of buyer or seller and the price point.

- Think like your target buyer and seller.

- Always include a CTA in your contact, on every marketing platform you use. Make it clear exactly what you want your prospect to do (call, email, click here, etc.)

Chapter Four
First Page or Bust

You know the optimal place, target audience, lead generation sources and selling points. Now it's time to build your online presence. If you do this part of your marketing right, it will prove to be the most lucrative way to build a seven-figure business!

Your Mega-Marketing plan should include two types of websites for your business — a Branded website (that builds the image of your company and supports your USP) and web pages that promote individual listings. Remember when I said at the beginning of this book that I would explain the difference between building your Brand and building your business. Well, here it is.

Building your Brand takes time. People go through a process that has been referred to as "Awareness/Acceptance/Action". First, you need to be found in content that motivates people to learn more about you and your business (Awareness). Then, it usually takes at least three times for them to read, register and believe your USP (Acceptance) before they will take an Action, like calling or clicking for more information.

Building your business, on the other hand, is more immediate. It's about bringing in prospects that are ready to buy or sell and want to work with you because of what you have available. As you've probably figured out, you build your Brand on your business website, through non-listing advertisements, Public Relations, etc. On the other hand, you build your business by promoting your properties.

Property Focused Websites

One of the best ways to promote your individual properties is to list them separately online. Get started on the right path by first exploring ePropertySites.com. The technology behind this property-marketing platform is remarkable and, along with ActiveRain, it is one of the key linchpins to launching your future success. As ePropertySites.com states, its mission is "Perfecting the Art of Property Marketing Online and Onsite."

The site was designed by a 'wizard' technology officer (with a portfolio that boasts Fortune 500 clients like Coca-Cola) in partnership with a veteran Real Estate Broker. This is definitely the website on which to showcase your properties, and then alert your target audience using the platform's Full-Screen Hi-Def and features like single property sites, virtual tours and posting tools.

When I coach Real Estate Agents, they get plenty of help setting up their home base on ePropertySites.com, including simple instructions for creating single property websites, choosing a layout and domain that is uniquely theirs, uploading photos and optimizing the site. I teach agents to maximize the value of several applications offered on the site, including those for music selection, selecting front page banners and identifying a spokesperson in sync with a company's style.

When you visit the site, you'll notice that the virtual tour, You Tube video and Google street view are all created automatically. In addition to the benefits described above, you can include property features. Plus, you'll get help deciding whether to create a blog post for an individual property website. The program will remind you to put keywords in as property features if you do decide to write a post. If you don't go for the blog post, you can still add features to the listing page, like a private pool or granite countertops. Finally, it's simple to activate the site.

Your Own Website

You will also want to increase your visibility on the Internet with a Wordpress-based business website that will work in partnership with ePropertySites.com. Wordpress is incredibly simple to use so you will be able to update your website quickly and efficiently yourself.

As with so many parts of developing your marketing materials, you don't have to do this alone. A few companies, with which I've worked, can make building and running your website a breeze. The first is www.iFoundAgent.com. It designs websites specifically for the Real Estate industry and will help you create an indexable IDX (so you can share your listings among different sites), make you mobile responsive and help you launch a simple yet sophisticated website with easy-to-add video and much more. In turn, IFoundAgent.com uses GetFound IDX, the first search engine-friendly IDX developed specifically for Word Press. It comes with the following features, which are important to developing a first-class, active website:

- Supports video on property details, city and neighborhood pages — allows you to create a specific video message for your ideal client or showcase a CTA as to why the visitor should call/email/or fill out a form on your website

- Creates pre-set searches for Short Sales, REOs, HUD Homes and many more options like Golf Properties, Horse Properties, etc.

- Indexable GetFound IDX integrated and custom setup specific to your website

- Indexable listings, city pages, neighborhood pages set up for maximum search ability and visibility

- No iframes

- IDX and website are optimized for "long tail" searches to attract more visitors

- No limit on the number of listings allowed per category

- Soft or Forced Registration form—not only for your IDX pages, but for the whole website

- State-of-the-art keyword search setup for IDX—allows you to customize your searches

- Synchronized with your MLS every 10 minutes

- Display listings based on your personal MLS ID and Broker's Office ID

- Quick Search tool

- Featured listings widget that displays up to six listings
- Advanced Search page

An Active, Live Website is Critical to Success

Why are the features above so important? It's because today's technological world demands a living, breathing, constantly changing website, not the old passive journal format of yesterday. Your potential customers are tech-savvy and demand the same expertise from you! If you don't set up your website with the right applications, you won't be able to access the data you need or allow mobile phone users to search and download material easily from your site.

You need video to record your introductory message – and, no, it can't just be written. People want to see you and hear you. Plus, it's a proven fact that visitors are more likely to stay on your site longer if there is video. You also need to anticipate the questions your targeted clients will have and create dynamic videos that provide the answers. Create links to ePropertySites.com where they can view all your current offerings, as well as other links to your blog on ActiveRain. Don't forget about adding those videos to your You Tube channel.

Remember, your website cannot be a static book. It must be an active, breathing, ongoing visual seminar that vibrates with your positive energy and signals that you can be trusted – you are a top ranking professional, a Real Estate superstar!

Search Marketing

Once your online presence is locked in, you will be ready to start implementing the principles of search marketing. Start by submitting your new business website to the various search engines, which is telling them you exist. Although Google is the most powerful search engine by far, you should also get set up with Yahoo, Bing, Lycos, AOL search, ask.com and mywebsearch.com. Ultimately, you'll also post to Craig's List twice a week, add blog posts at least once a week and employ other tactics to optimize SEO for both your own website and your eProperties.com listings.

When it comes to Google, there are countless experts out there dying to advise you for hefty fees. But, you certainly don't need them to get started. What you really need to know is the basics of how the Google ranking system works – the how, why and what. As we touched on in Chapter Two, Google uses a variety of methods to compute its "Google ranking." Many factors, from backend properties of your website to keyword placement, get evaluated, and a complex mathematical formula is used to determine each of your site's scores. Those scores are continually updated and used to determine what gets displayed in what order when the results of a keyword search are pulled up.

In order to move up in the rankings, you need to expand the number of times and places you show up on the web organically. The more places you appear (links to your website on other sites and mentions in listings) and the more frequently keywords are positioned properly on your own sites) the more Google will 'pick you up' while it is 'crawling the net.' Some other simple tips include sticking to one subject per page and prominently featuring one keyword or long-tailed keyword phrase per page. You can even name the pages of your website so that a keyword appears as part of the address line.

Should you find the whole subject daunting, not to worry. Consider working with a coach like myself who provides one-on-one training to implement the systems that will make you a star in the industry. Just please don't sign up with one of those 'Google experts,' as their whole purpose is to keep you coming back to them when you need something done. That's wasting money! When someone teaches you how to do things yourself, you can become a true master of the Internet, one who knowsthe secret to 'first page or bust!' And you can hire an assistant or outsource for blogging help to update your web presence on a regular basis.

Recap

- Create a web presence that includes ePropertySites.com for individual listings and a Wordpress business website to make your marketing fun and easy — that way you'll turn into an Internet whiz on your way to a 7-figure income in no time!

- Learn the rules and understand what's required to boost your Google rankings. Believe it or not, you can actually overuse keywords, and that hurts your rankings.

- Don't forget to include the other major search engines in your efforts.

Chapter Five

Choose Your Online Hub: Web vs. Social Media

Social media is rapidly changing the rules of the online marketing game. It used to be simple enough. As illustrated in the previous chapter, you built a website, made the content friendly for search engines, and it was a go. Today, social media—especially Facebook, with its billion members – is reshaping the future of marketing on the web. It is now important to look at why a website is fast becoming just one spoke on the online marketing wheel. The focus is increasingly on social media – how to use it to reach prospects, build your Brand and explode your lead generation capabilities.

Facebook condenses content into smaller, more manageable posts comprised of words, pictures or videos. It's easier for people to decide quickly if they are interested in what's being said. Facebook is too large to ignore. You simply have to be there. Even if you personally think it's a waste of time (and it is definitely a time suck for a lot of people), you must create and maintain a Facebook business page.

The first trick to using Facebook is determining what people will find interesting. Remember FORM and mix up your subject matter; don't just post listings. In that way, it is similar to your blog. The second trick is in knowing how much to include on your Facebook page and in your posts. That leads to the third trick, which is to direct them to your website or listings for more information and the collection of their contact information. Use acceptable promotions and offers (Facebook has some very strict rules) to build your follower base.

Facebook keeps innovating in its operations and functionality so that your fan page can include much of the best content once only possible on a freestanding website. Facebook is also making it easier for you to update fan pages without the services of an IT expert. As Facebook constantly makes enhancements to its proprietary Insights Analytics product, it's obvious that their goal is to give companies far more information about their visitors than Google Analytics – watch out big G! Finally, Facebook is winning the battle of push versus pull.

Personal vs. Business Pages

Now that you see the importance of social media and, in particular, Facebook, you are probably wondering what the difference is between a business page and a personal page in Facebook. Here's the basic difference, according to Facebook:

Personal Pages

- Are meant to be used to connect with people you know in real life, although many business people interact with each other and clients via teir personal pages
- Represent you, the person
- Much better for social communication and to build relationships
- Can be used to invite friends to join your business page
- Are meant for non-commercial use, but the restrictions are vague and are constantly changing. Again, business people often use their personal page to talk about their business. However, they rarely include promotional offers, coupons, etc.
- Can connect with other people, join groups or play social games

Business Pages

- Are used to build your Brand and communicate with current clients, as well as potential ones
- Represent your company as a whole
- Are used to manage ad campaigns, run contests and promotions
- Can be used on conjunction with your personal page to reach more people within your niche
- Can place ads and alo pay Facebook to boost posts for larger reach in readership
- Can't be found in search, nor send or receive friend requests
- Can see public information about other people on Facebook, but can't interact with those people except as a Page
- Can't engage in social games, although you can now comment on someone's personal page as your business page

You Tube

First, learn to love video, and not just video of the houses you are showing. While you might want to create video especially for your website, most of this section of the chapter is about how to set up an account on the most popular video site today – You Tube. No matter the size of your company – even if you are just starting up – video is the closest thing to face-to-face contact.

The first step is to create a You Tube account with an email address. Try and create one with your business name in it, as it will be the name of the channel also. Connect your website and You Tube accounts through links and educate your target clients on why they need your services. You can illustrate in a video exactly how you can help them find their dream home or that investment property they have been busily searching for on their own.

Add a message to the end of your videos asking viewers to subscribe to your channel so they'll see every video that you post. Include a sign-up on the home page of your website and your Facebook page.

Promote Social Media Accounts Everywhere

You've just had a glimpse of how social media can promote your business. To make it work, you will need to promote your presence on those social media sites to build a following for your business. Start by including a 'follow me' app on your website and your Facebook business page. Also, include all your social media information in your email signature, in printed pieces, at the bottom of newsletters, etc. The point is simple: make it easy for people to find you and follow you.

Encourage new followers through promotions and gifts. As mentioned previously, Facebook alters its rules on sweepstakes and promotions regularly, so check them before running any special efforts to attract new followers. As with other lead generation tactics, free information is a good gift for signing up... and it doesn't really cost you anything (especially as you can deliver it electronically).

Maximize Your Facebook Presence

One of the most important strategies for all of your online efforts involves engagement; that is getting prospects to visit your website and Facebook business page often. In addition to regularly updating your listings use your online presence —especially your Facebook page — to keep your followers engaged with your Brand. Include actual informational content on the page and post that there is news on your page. Facebook advertising is also a very effective tool for promoting your business page. Make sure that you track results for ROI, change your 'creative' (ad) and test which messages do best at generating leads and return visitors.

If you want your followers to stay engaged, you must first be engaged with them. So, don't forget to socialize — people want to get to know you. Use your posts to enhance your image and promote your USP by being human. Let them know when your kids do something special, when there is something happening in your area (school fairs, high school sports wins, etc.). You'll also want to share stories about satisfied clients, re-post others' comments, etc. Just make certain that your posts are a mix of personal and listings. Don't be all business all the time as that's not how social media works.

My Digital Media Blog

An automated blogging and social media solution, My Digital Media Blog (http://mydigitalmediablog.com) creates a fresh Real Estate article every business day of the month, and posts it directly to a Wordpress blog created for you. That post is then immediately sent out to the social media accounts of your choosing. This tool can be a lifesaver for those who do not fully understand social media and need a jump start to their own efforts. My Digital Media Blog also saves the average Realtor about 25 hours per month of content creation. That's seven weeks per year!

Tracking is Essential

Use the lead tracker form in the Appendix of this book to ensure that you appropriately follow up on every lead you get. By appropriate I mean that you should know which response mechanism is preferred: email, phone, face-to-face, printed materials. Make sure to collect all the data cited on the form and leave room for notes to yourself.

Keep your form updated after every contact. Yes, it's paperwork, and may seem time consuming, but tracking is everything in the Real Estate business. Never let a lead get lost in the crowd. It is best to use a customer relationship management (CRM) or database management system like Wise Agent or Top Producer. Wise Agent is much simpler and easier than the others are to start with, but any CRM will work; Real Estate-specific programs make things easier.

Putting It All Together

If you've got the impression that this sounds like a lot of work, or are unclear about what happens first, second or third, not to worry. Here's just one example of how the communication between you and a lead might play out.

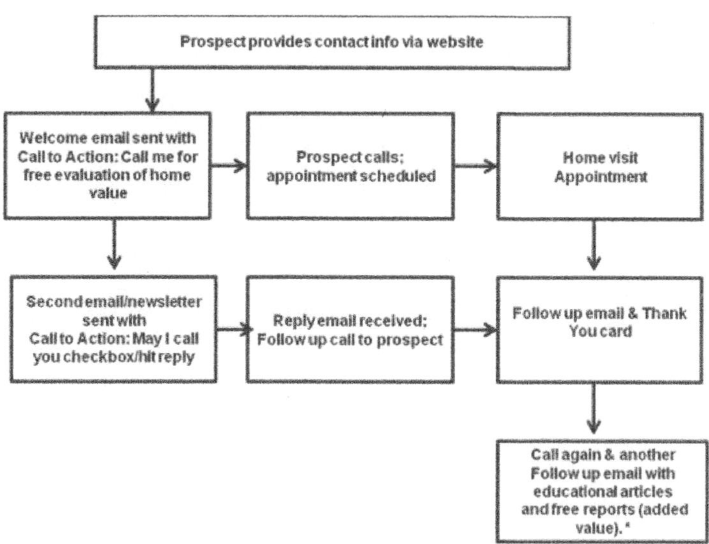

Recap

- You must have a real online presence. That includes a Branded website, listings via eProperties and a blog on ActiveRain.

- Social media can be your friend. Posting is easy, and it gives you the opportunity to let your target audience know who you are. That is as a person, as well as a brand.

- In the case of online, familiarity breeds respect and relationships. Engage your target audience often everywhere you have an online presence.

- Every website and social media site is a lead generator.

- Build your social media follower base through promotions and gifts, especially free information that proves you are an expert in your area.

- Learn to love video. In addition to your You Tube channel, use video on your website. Remember that it is a great way to update your website. Plus, Google scans for video.

Chapter Six
Getting on the List

You probably get most of your clients from personal recommendations, so you know how critical they are in the Real Estate market. Imagine what it would be like if you could increase your referrals by tenfold. How about twentyfold or more? Well, that's what happens when you can be found on a referral list.

Being on the right lists is another goal for a Real Estate Mega-Agent – and the two most important ones can be found online. You are likely already familiar with them as they are widely-used household names: Craig's List and Angie's List.

Launched back in 1995, Craig's List was once considered an internet phenomenon. It is now the go-to place for both individuals and businesses to buy, sell, locate and advertise just about anything. The other, Angie's List, is more recent but is already cultivating a reputation for reliability, in part through its advertising tagline, "reviews you can trust."

Craig's List

Craig's List is one of the true legends of the Internet. It started as an email list of San Francisco events but soon morphed into a nationwide (customized by location) website with more than 50 billion page views per month. It is used by more than 60 million people each month in the US alone. Originally, the founder focused on local classifieds and forums, made the site community moderated and largely free. Incorporated as a for-profit in 1999, Craig's List has kept its.org domain and continues to thrive although there are more instances in which a fee is involved.

As a Real Estate Agent, another important thing to remember is that Craig's List posts well over 100 million classified ads each month (including reposts and renewals). It has little to no competition; Craig's List not only beats all competitors in every category, it also garners more traffic than all of them combined. This is a natural rainmaker, and you need to have a strong presence. Open several accounts, build a dynamic Craig's List profile for each and post multiple ads per account (shoot for at least twice a week). It may sound like a lot of work, but there are ways to post your listings in seconds. (Check out www.youtube.com/user/bizcoachaz to find out how you can learn the same tips and tools I share with my consulting clients.) We'll also teach you how to manipulate the code to add your IDX link for further searchability.

Angie's List

Your second most important list is Angie's List. The concept behind the website is to certify their data collection process by only allowing paid and registered subscribers to access the website. This is done to discourage anonymous or biased reviews. According to the site, members submit more than 60,000 reviews every month about the companies (including Real Estate agencies) they hire. The reviews grade response time, price, professionalism and quality of work on an A to F scale. Angie's List reports having more than two million paid households as members throughout the US.

So how do you fit in? As a businessperson, you can register free on the Angie's List Business Center website at www.angieslistbusinesscenter.com. The site offers a full range of tools to help you broadcast your superior service. Remember that your placement on Angie's List is controlled by grades and reviews from members – and only Angie's List members can give your business grades. However, as a business member, you can read and respond to reviews on your agency. In fact, the site encourages you to respond because Angie's List members will often look at a company's response before they make their hiring decision.

There is a wide variety of easy-to-use tools offered by the Business Center, many of them free. The tools allow you to maximize results by letting your member testimonials speak for you. These tools and promotional products make it easy for you to build your review base. You can:

- Collect reviews with free, postage-paid forms for your clients

- Print your forms for free or order customized, color copies

- Include tear pads with invoices or an appointment reminder

- Show clients you want feedback with an electronic badge by placing the badge on your website and using it in emails

- You can also get/use:

    - Smaller forms and stickers that contain your customized review link

    - A free, customized link directing clients to submit reviews online — use it on invoices, stationary and business cards.

The founders of Angie's List promise their most highly rated providers ways to maximize exposure. Once you've established your presence and started collecting reviews, you can become an A or B rated provider (with at least two current reviews) and, as such, eligible to advertise and extend exclusive offers and deals to Angie's List members. The site promises that taking advantage of these opportunities exponentially increases your exposure to members looking for quality providers like you.

Strategic Partner Lists

If you've heard about strategic partner and joint venture business arrangements before, you probably assumed that they were just for big businesses and corporations. They're not. Strategic partners can be essential to building your business, and finding and working with them is easy.

Earlier in the book you saw how important it is to learn as much as you can about your target prospects so you will know where and how to market to them. If you haven't already done so, brainstorm about who is your ideal client target. What kinds of activities do they engage in, where do they shop, etc. For example, if you are going after the luxury market, you might assume that they are more likely than the average homeowner is to take trips, entertain, collect wine, belong to the country club and play golf.

The information you've collected gives you a perfect start for building your strategic partner list. So does your own life.

Establishing a Network Database

You already have a network in the other professionals you or your clients work with — attorneys, mortgage brokers, accountants, etc. That's the nucleus upon which to build your list of strategic partners. Here's what it looks like:

There's a simple process to follow when pulling together a database of people in your network:

- Begin with a close, small area, working within a five-mile radius of your home or office.
- Start with the businesses you frequent (remember that you are a lot like your target prospect). Include doctors, dentists, landscapers, gyms, dry cleaners, restaurants and other places where you shop.
- Find similar markets with similar clientele. You may find your zip code and subdivision analysis extremely helpful in identifying potential partners.

- Make sure to offer a benefit to the business you are approaching — it might be coupon placement within your promotional or educational materials or on the web. Brainstorm with your strategic partners to determine the best reciprocity of efforts.

- Develop a Follow-Up Drip System of communications with and about your strategic partners. Always relate your messaging back to what your prospects, buyers and sellers, want and need. (More about Drip Marketing in the next chapter.)

Recap

- Online lists like Craig's List and Angie's List are the equivalent of client referrals on steroids.

- Keep track of what people are saying about you and your company so that you can control the conversation about your Brand. On Angie's List, that means responding to any negative comments on a timely basis.

- There are plenty of opportunities for strategic partnerships right near where you live and work. Start at the closest local level, and then branch out into nearby communities, looking to partner with businesses that appeal to your target audience.

- Remember that a strategic partnership works only if both companies get something out of the arrangement. Develop marketing materials and programs that are beneficial to both you and your partner business.

Chapter Seven
Blogging & Email Marketing

Online marketing is an especially efficient way to reach your target audience. You can identify qualified targets and market to them at a much lower cost than using direct marketing materials like brochures. So, get those creative juices flowing so you can put your marketing message out there using blogging and email. Both are important vehicles for reaching your target audience, but your content may vary depending on which format you are writing for. Let's start with blogging.

Blogging

Once you have set up your blog on ActiveRain, you will be ready to start generating professional referrals from 320,000+ members active in Real Estate or related fields. You will also be able to contact two million homebuyers and sellers each month with your RainMaker account from ActiveRain.com.

As explained earlier, ActiveRain was constructed so each blog or webpage that goes live stays under the Activerain.com umbrella. That means when a blog is written, it feeds one domain name, thereby exponentially increasing your probability of making page one of a Google search for Real Estate in your area. This represents an extraordinary opportunity for your business. As Barbara Altieri, Realtor, Fairfield County CT Real Estate (RealtyQuest, Fairfield and New Haven County CT Homes for Sale and Real Estate) said on the website:

"Hyperlocal blogging about local neighborhoods and condo complexes has proven to be an ace in the hole for me. Here's a recent example. ONE, yes ONE post, on ONE community produced THREE, yes THREE new purchases in a three-week timeframe. Also, when you blog about local areas, you enrich your knowledge of those areas and likely learn more about them; hence, you are a wealth of knowledge to potential buyers. Hyperlocal is a WIN-WIN for Agents and buyers/sellers alike." Again, you can get started on ActiveRain by signing up at the following link, http://activerain.com/action/signup. (See http://activerain.com/getting-started for a recap of the procedures and guidelines.)

Creating Blog Posts

For inspiration, look at what other Real Estate Agents are doing on ActiveRain. What stands out? What blogs get you to pause a moment in your busy day? What posts might be of special interest to your clients and prospects? Then, remember the acronym FORM: family, occupation, recreation and money. Those are topics that everyone can relate to, and never get tired of reading about.

Generally, think of family getaways your potential clients would enjoy, money-saving tips on heating or renovations, work-life balance or changing careers midlife (and how that might affect the way one uses space within the home). If your business is near some large corporations or in a business cluster (like pharmaceutical companies in the state of New Jersey), you might get a lot of fodder writing about professions related to that industry. Overall, you will find lots of information online once you starting researching ideas. Remember that what appeals to you will also appeal to your readers.

Headlines are important for garnering readership. People tend to love tips, numbers and statements that jump off the page. For instance, Redfin, a company comprised of Real Estate Agents and software engineers, had a blog post with the headline, "If Dorothy was a Chimp, She'd Wear Red Cowboy Boots: What Redfin Learned at Chimpanzee Sanctuary Northwest." Could you really resist clicking on that link? It's a great story about a delightful sanctuary your audience might enjoy visiting, especially if they are already in the Northwest.

On the other end of the spectrum, Realty Biz News (realitybiznews.com) posted "7 Quick-and-easy-ways-to-add-curb-appeal," with simple ideas like cleaning the windows. Tips like these also draw readership because they include information the reader can use to make their home more sellable. Readers also love when you answer client or prospect questions in a blog post; if some are frequently asked questions, make the most of them by creating content for your blog or an email.

Once you've written a few posts, you'll find yourself getting faster and better at doing so. In a pinch, just quickly put together your own original blog with references to the source, (ex: I just read about a chimp sanctuary you must visit on your next trip to the Northwest) or direct your audience to the online article, post or information site.

In terms of timing, you need not post every day, but you should set up a schedule that includes at least one blog post a week. You can always up or reduce the number of blog entries a month, but you need to be consistent. If you are not sure how often to post, see what other people are doing on ActiveRain. For solid activity and leads, you should post once/day or schedule posts to hit each day.

Email Marketing

In addition to blogging, you should be designing a 'drip' marketing campaign, again using the topics in FORM to relate to your target audience. The term drip simply refers to a steady series of communications. Two examples of drip email marketing are a monthly newsletter and a five-part series on fixing up your home for sale (with an email a week). A third example involves sending out a quick email to your list letting them know you've just posted a new blog entry; you will find it useful in promoting your blog.

With email marketing, you can customize your content based on the type of people you are contacting. For example, one month you may send out a list of tips to sellers and an announcement of new listings to potential buyers. Other times, the same content will be relevant to all the people on your list, like when talking about a community event, your family vacation, etc. And, yes, you do want to mix personal messages into your email and blog communications. People want to get to know you! You don't have to make the entire post or email personal, but an observation or 'while we were away visiting the kids for Winter break' can go a long way to humanizing you and your business.

A Word About Direct Mail

Online communications are your most cost-efficient way to reach a large number of people in your target niche, but that doesn't mean you should stop using printed materials altogether. Postcards and brochures will always have a place in your marketing mix, especially when working with strategic partners, advertising a successful sale or announcing a new property for sale. The point is to focus on online messaging and make it an integral part of your marketing and brand building. Of course, it's important to project your brand image consistently and to reinforce your message in several areas:

- Face-to-face as you meet potential and current clients

- By phone whenever you reach out or take incoming inquiries

- By email, making sure your blog postings go directly to your target audience

- Direct mail, targeting audiences by region or zip code with current offerings

Recap

- Set up your blog on ActiveRain and post consistently .

- Go beyond your listings to blog about ideas and topics that will hook your target audience.

- Remember to check for comments that need addressing or questions that require an answer. Use the comments section to reply to very specific questions or to thank someone for their comments. Create full blog posts for questions with mass appeal.

- Use email to call attention to your blog, as well as to deliver helpful hints, information about new listings and strategic partner promotions. Don't forget to include a link to your eproperties site.

- Extend the reach of your marketing message through email and direct mail so that you effectively implement a drip marketing campaign, constantly reinforcing your brand image and competitive advantages.

- Now you are really rolling! Start saturating the Internet with your presence and build an audience for your properties. You are ready to turn this treasure trove into actual sales success!

- Congratulations on choosing the victor mode, with the qualities of ownership, accountability and responsibility. By the way, FEAR often keeps realtors where they are because it stands for "False Expectations Appearing Real." Get ready to win!

Chapter 8
Make Time for Marketing & Success

Now that you know what has to be done to transform your Real Estate business into a mega-marketing success, are you ready to get started? Don't worry if it sounds a bit daunting; there are lots of tools to make you more efficient and effective, especially in implementing your marketing program, lead generation and follow-through.

If you haven't already done so, create your target audience profile using the recommended form. Then, develop your 90-day action plan (see Chapter Two and the Appendix for a template).

Use your marketing planning and strategies worksheets, remembering to include all the marketing tools you plan to use. Get specific. List the associated tasks that need to get done each week with due dates. Then, commit to implementing that plan. Keep track of completion dates and review your results every month.

Stick to Your Strategic Plan

It's so easy to wander off the path to your goals. Time wasters lie in wait each day, and you have to remember the importance of implementing a strategic plan faithfully if you want to keep your business growing instead of stagnating.

You can't just squeeze your marketing tasks into your day. You must make them a priority and schedule time to work on building your business. To do that, you need to eliminate unnecessary tasks and delegate others. The goal is to put your focus on the productive areas of your business and hire a great team to handle the rest. The process sounds simple enough, but the inability to streamline and delegate is the Achilles heel for many otherwise smart and ambitious Real Estate Agents.

The most brilliant strategic plan will fail if your focus in not razor sharp. If you faithfully use my 90-day plan, you'll be running full-speed in three months. Your job after that is to keep evaluating and updating your plan every 90 days. How simple is that?

Stay Organized

Sticky notes can either be your best friend or your undoing. Don't use scraps of paper when there's a form that can keep you organized and on track. In this book, you will find sample forms that can make the 'drudge' work fast and simple. Plus, you'll be certain you are collecting all the information you need at the same time when the form is right at hand. Going back to get more information from someone you've already spoken with is one of the biggest time wasters I know. Plus, it makes you look less professional to your prospects.

Keep It Simple

Systems and forms are meant to help you, not add more work. The simpler they are, the better. For example, are you one of those people who keep more than one calendar? Perhaps you have a hard copy calendar, an online calendar, a social calendar, a separate calendar for your family and lists of monthly meetings tacked on a bulletin board or the refrigerator. Or, worse still, no calendar at all —just lots of small pieces of paper and stickies? If so, you are bound to miss appointments, overbook your time, be constantly late and generally live in chaos on a regular basis.

Here are just a few of the tools I recommend to my coaching clients:

Keep One Calendar

You need a default calendar —one calendar on which you organize everything. Yes, everything from business appointments to doctor visits, school activities and client moving dates. It's all one life, hence one calendar. Many business people like to use their Google or Outlook calendars as their default calendars while others prefer one on their website. You should choose a location that makes it easy to add invitations to meetings and content from emails directly to the calendar.

Make Lists

Do you have a to-do list? If not, start one. You can't expect yourself to keep everything that has to be done in your head. Lists are also strong organizational tools for mapping out all the steps that have to be done for an Open House, closing, or marketing effort. Just make sure that your lists don't end up having lists of their own — in other words, don't complicate things and, certainly, don't spend all your time making lists rather than completing the items on them.

Use your ABCs

Have you ever had so many things to do that you couldn't decide which one to do first? That's what happens when all tasks are loosely put into a list without determining their importance. Prioritizing to-do's is an excellent way to keep yourself on track. The ABC List is a standard organizational tool for keeping you on track. Assign an "A" for urgent and time-sensitive tasks, "B" to the other things that need to get done that week and a "C" to those to-dos that are the least important, or have the longest due date. (Never record a to-do without assigning it a due date. You can always delay something if you have to, but non-dated tasks have a tendency to fall off the list).

Use a Points System

Set up a 'point sales system' that ranks each of your prospecting and marketing activities by importance and urgency to act. You may base it on hours spent, number of calls made, etc. Once you allocate a set number of points to a prospecting activity, you can determine how many times you do that activity to keep track of how you are spending your time.

For example, you should be spending two to three hours a day prospecting, either talking to people face-to-face or on the phone. So, assign a value-based amount of points into your system for that overall purpose. That will ensure that you talk to and meet up with enough people to hit your desired results.

The points system is an essential management tool that will help make sure you are staying top-of-mind on a timely basis, that is communicating with current clients and hot prospects who might be in the buying cycle, while not 'talking' to someone else so much that you actually turn them off. Regularly confirm that you are communicating the proper number of times with everyone in your database.

The points system also aids in increasing the profitability of your marketing activities, especially when using printed materials (which are much more expensive than email marketing). Just make sure you account for each communication or 'points earned' with each contact.

The idea is to help you achieve your goals in managing your clients for the most profitability.

Set Up Your RAS – 'I am' Statements

What are your weaknesses that you would like to get rid of in your life? What areas of your life and characteristics you would like to see strengthen? This is a simple but very important process. You make a list of 21 "I am" statements, some of which are true, but represent characteristics that could be improved or would help you even more if applied more often. The examples below should give you a great start. You need to read your list for five minutes in the morning and again for five minutes at night before bed.

I AM ...

1. A loving, kind, respectful woman to all others

2. A role model to my children

3. A consistent and focused woman

4. Confident in myself and my abilities

5. An empowered woman

6. Fearless in business and new ventures

7. A healthy person of body, mind, and spirit

8. Creative with my business and finding solutions

9. Inspiring to other women
10. Successful in helping others achieve results
11. A successful nationally known speaker
12. A successful nationally known author
13. In control of my thoughts, decisions, choices, and time on task
14. A great mother, loving wife, aunt, and best friend
15. A woman that focuses on constant learning every day
16. A woman that is self-motivated and determined to succeed in business
17. Financially responsible for helping my family
18. A woman determined to make a $100,000 in one year
19. A positive person that surrounds herself with positive people
20. A woman in control of her own life
21. A person that creates successful life changing products for others

Delegate

You don't have to do every little thing yourself. Trust me, you are not the only one who can file or fill out papers, put up 'For Sale' signs or look up target audience data. Of course, you should be the one to do the things that require your expertise, but it's easy to delegate the rest.

Think you can't afford to hire someone? The truth is you can't afford not to. Keep in mind that you are leaving 'money on the table' every hour you do 'grunt work' instead of marketing. If you're not devoting half of your time to building your business, you are doing yourself and your company a huge disservice.

The best way to quantify your time is by deciding how much money you want to make in the next 12 months. Let's say you want to make $150,000. Take that figure and divide it by 2,080 to determine the value of every one of your hours based on that $150,000 goal. By doing this, you will see your time is worth $72/hour.

Then, you need to make yourself a to-do list with all of the things you do in a given day. Make sure to include the items you want and like to do that make you money. Then, make a 'Not to-do' list. This is a list of the things that you don't like, that stress you out and on which you wish you didn't have to do and waste your time. This 'NOT to-do' list encompasses the tasks you currently do in a day that you would NOT pay someone $72/hour to do. These things waste valuable time and money because you are doing them yourself.

The key strategy for moving items to the 'Not to-do' list is that, for every item you remove off your to-do list (which is making you less than $72/hour), add a high dollar value activity or high life improvement activity on the to-do list. That way, you will continue to produce greater results and a better you while maximizing your dollar-per-hour activities and your money.

Hold Yourself Accountable

Having a coach or an accountability partner keeps you focused and on track better than you can on your own. He or she can keep you motivated, with your mind centered on the big picture, so you don't lose sight of the things that matter the most – what you truly want to have in life and business. A coach works with you to make the life you dream of happen, and that's critical because if you wait for it to happen, it won't.

For example, as a coach I take my clients through a proven process to answer this crucial question: What does your ideal life and business look, feel, smell, taste and sound like? You need to get a clear picture in order to shape it for yourself, and working with the right person can help you do just that.

An experienced coach can also help you refine your marketing plans and strategies to fit your business and area of opportunity. Unlike most Real Estate Agents, who are on a roller coaster ride to nowhere, you can learn how to create and implement a business plan that is truly right for you and your business based on where you are now and where you want to be in the future.

I also counsel my clients so they can change their behaviors to become more productive and let go of their need to do everything themselves. We develop a Business Roadmap, a plan of action that fits the "haves" they want. Just as a real roadmap will help you get geographically from California to Michigan, a customized Business Roadmap will help you get from where you are now to where you want to go as a mega-Real Estate Agent.

Recap

- Keep on plan, making to-do lists to record tasks. Check to see that all are complete on a timely basis.

- Prioritize tasks using the A, B, C method. Don't forget to change a to-do's priority as its due date approaches.

- Use a point system to keep track of your communications per contact.

- Automate your database and keep it current. Use the information to refine your marketing activities for maximum impact and profitability.

- Use forms to simplify tasks and ensure you collect all the information you need for each contact or project.

- Delegate! Your time is too valuable to use it tending to $10 and $12 an hour tasks.

- Get a coach — the right coach — to help you be accountable for your own success and achieve the life of which you dream.

Chapter 9
Consistent Growth

Unlike the ups and downs you've most likely been experiencing in your business, you can achieve consistent growth and profits. You can make six figures a year, or much more. And, you now know how to get yourself there.

You must promote your USP and build your target audience base by consistently marketing your business as well as your listings. In the previous chapters, you've seen how critical the Internet has become to building your Real Estate business, and you've learned how to use it effectively on a local basis. You've also been given some management tools to help put together a successful plan of action and implement it on a regular basis.

Consistency of action is the key to constant growth. Remember that all your actions have two common purposes: to find qualified prospects and to close properties. Here's a recap of the top ways to turn your Real Estate business into a mega-marketing success.

Always Be Generating Leads

Everything you do should be a lead generator, especially in terms of your marketing efforts:

- Give people a reason to provide their contact information by offering free information about purchasing or selling Real Estate, news about their neighborhood or fun facts about the hobbies and activities they enjoy.

- Make it easy for people to subscribe to your blog or email list. Use sign-up boxes online, coupons in printed materials and other forms that simplify the process for your prospects.

- Build a substantial database using an online CRM program like Act or Wise Agent, which are Internet-based business management systems that Real Estate professionals use daily. Pick one that you find easy to use (and to teach to a part-timer or assistant) so that you never fall behind in entering prospect information into the database.

- Your list is your most valuable business-building tool, so use it wisely. Customize communications, test headlines and update a contact's status regularly (had a phone call, became a client, recommended to others).

Engage, Engage, Engage

Communication shouldn't be a one-way street. The more you learn about your prospects, the more equipped you will be to provide exactly what they are looking for. Remember the acronym FORD, a variation of FORM where the 'D' stands for dreams. Encourage your prospects and clients to share their goals and describe their dream house.

Your blog and newsletters are perfect vehicles for collecting this information. Build your readership by promoting your blog everywhere you can, make it easy to subscribe to your newsletter and encourage current readers to forward the email on to a friend, etc.

People love posts and e-articles that encourage dialog, so ask questions about the topic you are writing about or suggest that people send you questions that can be answered in a later post. Also, when you talk about something in your own life (vacations, the first day at school, how we coped during the storm), ask readers to share similar experiences or provide tips that can be shared with your list.

Always Be Closing

I don't have to tell you that there is a path from prospect to client and from looking at a property to closing on it. Every time you move someone further along the path you are, in some way, closing. So, every action you take should have a next step that moves someone down that path. Always include a CTA in your marketing materials, one that keeps moving the potential buyer towards becoming a client, a current client to a new homeowner or satisfied seller, and past clients to future clients when the time is right (and to recommend you to others).

This is where customized message streams and content come into play. In addition to your more general newsletters and new listing notices, you should have an email campaign for each type of prospect or client. How often you email each type comes out of your points' analysis. Here's an example of how it works at the most simple level:

- Someone subscribes to your newsletter.

- You send an email thanking them for subscribing and remind them of the things they will get or learn from future newsletters and emails.

- They go into your normal email stream as a long-term prospect.

- This person responds to one of the free information offers in your newsletter.

- You email them the information or, better still, provide a link to your website where they can immediately download the information. (Use a separate web page for this, so you can include a headline and some body copy that relate to the specific offer. Also, include links to follow you on the various social media sites.)

- You note in your database file that they responded to that particular offer.

- About a week after they get the download, you send a short email asking if they have had a chance to read the information and if they have any questions about it. Remember to include an email hyperlink in the content of your email, as well as your phone number. Again, you want it to be as easy as possible for them to contact you!

- You keep them in your normal communications stream and periodically send them emails offering more free information.

An Open House makes for another useful example of how to create interest, identify leads and begin moving them down the path towards qualified prospects and current clients.

- You start with a 'pre-Open House' period in which you knock on neighbors' doors and let them know that they are welcome to stop by on the day of the Open House, usually about an hour before the official start time, so you can answer any questions they may have. You start collecting contact information on each person with whom you speak.

- You don't stop there. On the day of the Open House, when these neighbors stop by, you offer a quick tour of the house to show how you helped the owner 'spiff' it up to sell for a higher price. You also ask if you can add them to your mailing or newsletter list. (Guess who that neighbor will list with when they are ready to sell their home?)

- Of course, you have done your homework beforehand so when visitors to the Open House ask about amenities, taxes and school rankings, you can verbally provide a general answer to their questions and offer to send them more details. At the minimum, you collect names and email addresses in order to send a more detailed answer to their questions.

- You also have a compelling flyer and your business cards near the door to encourage newsletter subscriptions and requests for free information (about selling prices in their area to appeal to the neighbors, other listings in the neighborhood to entice prospects, and so on).

DESIREABLE, fast moving neighborhood
quickly increasing in value...

Do you know what your home is worth?

For A Free Report on Home Values in Carmel Bay.

Name:

Address:

Phone:

Email:

- The day after the Open House, you send out a thank you to everyone who attended the event. Each of your emails is customized to include the information you promised, follow up on specific questions or direct prospects to one of your websites to see other listings in the area.

- You add every new contact into your database, including as much information as you can about who they are and what interests they have. Look to the form provided elsewhere in this book, as it is a terrific guide to what information you should be collecting. Many of my coaching clients find it helpful to have blank forms on hand at the Open House so they can fill out the paperwork while talking to the new prospect. They then turn the completed forms over to an assistant who enters the information into the database. Make sure the forms have an offer on them and a CTA for them to want to leave the information and get the FREE item. Some of the valuable items you can offer are FREE home evaluations or a valuable FREE report offering key information.

Here is a link from *Realtor.org* magazine and the National Association of Realtors (NAR) that offers over 30 reports you can download for FREE —www.realtormag.realtor.org. Click on the sales and marketing tab on the top of the page, then go to the bottom of the page and click on "Handouts for Customers." Download all 30+ reports created by the NAR and use them in your educational marketing and for direct response CTAs, especially in your open houses and direct mail/ flyers, etc.

Make the title of the report compelling; if NAR's are not, then change their titles and personal the reports to fit you!

- Based on the points system, you add each new contact into your communications stream. Voila! You also create a separate mailing list so that you can customize follow-up emails to remind these prospects how and when they met you.

Recap

- Consistent marketing is the key to achieving your dreams.

- View every marketing activity and event as an opportunity to generate new leads and move the closing process along.

- The more you know about a contact, the more successful you will be in closing the sale.

Chapter 10
Summing Up

You are now ready to stop worrying about the ups and downs of the Real Estate market and start marketing your business for mega results. I've given you the tools to start building a Mega-Marketing Real Estate business that can successfully compete in the current environment by using all the latest tools in the Real Estate Agent's toolbox. Your business can, and will, provide you with a six or seven-figure income. Get ready to fulfill your dreams!

Start by determining where your greatest potential lies (your target audience) and learn where and how to reach those people. Use the Internet and electronic media to encourage those target prospects to self-identify and provide their contact information. Know what will motivate them to buy or sell and create an image that builds off your USP. Then, convert those leads into qualified prospects and hot, ready-to-go sellers and buyers by providing a reason why your target clients should work with you — and only you.

Balance your time so that you focus on prospecting for at least 50% of your average day. Streamline or delegate other activities, so you don't get bogged down in the details. Remember that your time is worth a lot of money and that you really can't afford to do everything yourself.

Develop and implement systems that continuously generate warm leads and use a database program that can help identify when those leads are ready to become serious prospects or clients, then go out and close them.

And, never forget that you don't have to go it alone. Having a coach or accountability partner can help you become more successful than you ever imagined. The right coach can keep you on track, help simplify your processes and provide valuable strategic and tactical insights that will help you become a Mega-Real Estate Marketer in no time.

Appendix

MLS Chart 1

First Zip Code, Active & UCB

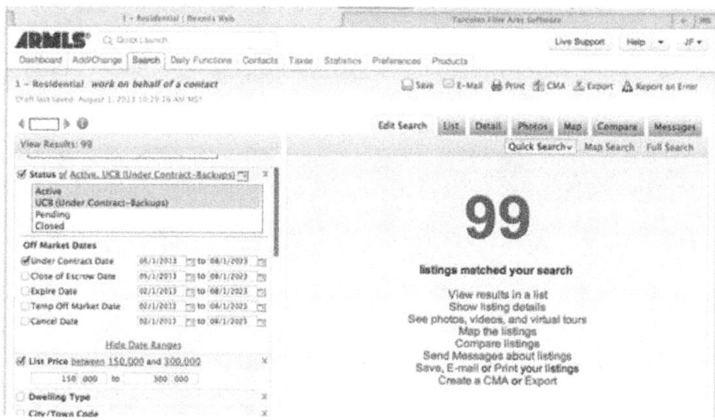

MLS Chart 2

First Zip Code Pending/Closed

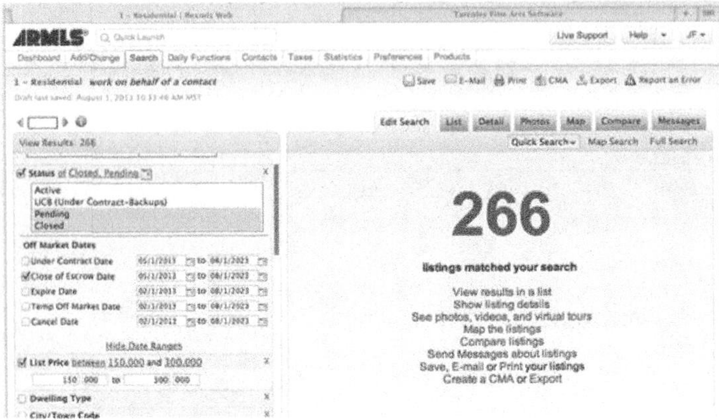

MLS Chart 3

2nd Zip Code Pending & Closed

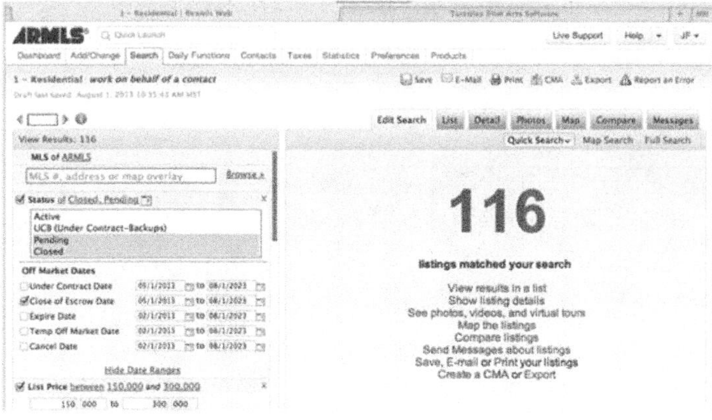

MLS Chart 4

2nd Zip Code Active & UCB

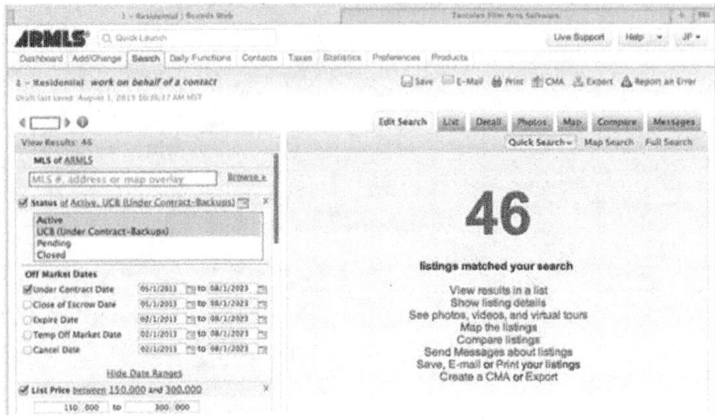

MLS Chart 5

Find Top Subs For Best Data Box

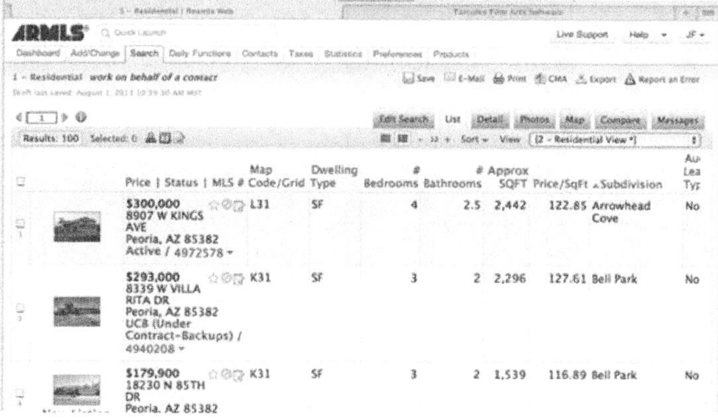

Target Market Data for ____________________ In ________________

(Agent Name) (Area/ Zip code/ Location)

Actives & UC - Pendings/Closed from _________ to __________

(Dates no more than 3 to 4 months BACK)

Price Range Subdivision/ Zipcodes	150K-300K	300K-450K	450K-600K	600K-750K	>750K
Totals					

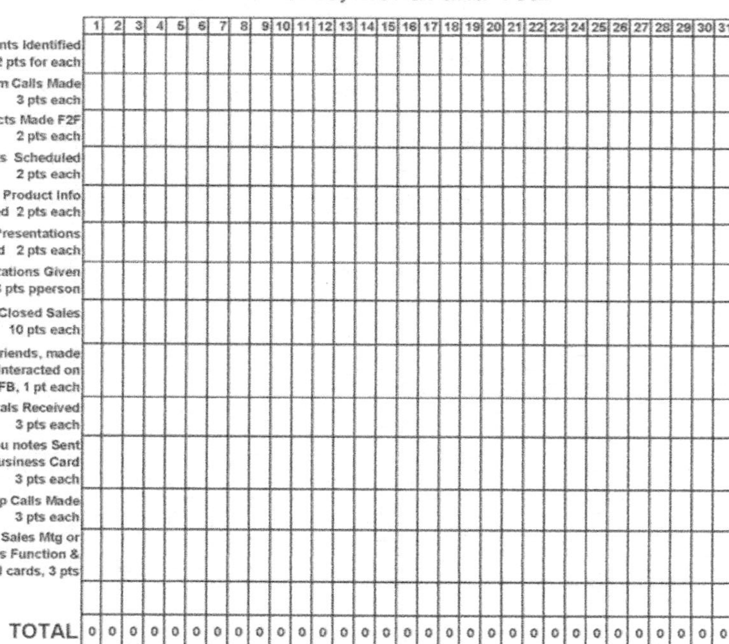

Daily Activity Graph
Name, Month and Year

	1	2	3	4	5	6	7	8	9	10	11	12	13	14	15	16	17	18	19	20	21	22	23	24	25	26	27	28	29	30	31
New Clients Identified & in DB 2 pts for each																															
Warm Calls Made 3 pts each																															
Contacts Made F2F 2 pts each																															
Visits/Mtgs Scheduled 2 pts each																															
Product Info Distributed 2 pts each																															
Presentations Prepared 2 pts each																															
Presentations Given 3 pts pperson																															
Closed Sales 10 pts each																															
Added friends, made posts & interacted on FB, 1 pt each																															
Referrals Received 3 pts each																															
Thank you notes Sent w/ Business Card 3 pts each																															
Follow Up Calls Made 3 pts each																															
Attended Sales Mtg or Business Function & collected cards, 3 pts																															
TOTAL	0	0	0	0	0	0	0	0	0	0	0	0	0	0	0	0	0	0	0	0	0	0	0	0	0	0	0	0	0	0	0

Lead Tracker Form

Lead Sheet Assigned To:	New Leads	Phone	Lead Source	Type	# Calls	JComp	JCoach	Purpose	FB/LI Notes	Notes

RLTR = Realtor PF = Personal Friend PCR = Past Client CCR = Current Client Referral BP = Business Partner
DM = Direct Mail AD = Advertisement JRLTR = Joey Realtor JREF = Joey Referral

In Processing										
Pre-Approved										
30 - 90 Days										
Out										
3 - 8 Months Out